Pot Luck

Living the dream in the West Country

by

Jennifer Bell

'POT LUCK'
By
Jennifer Bell

Copyright © 2015

ISBN: 978-0-9934032-0-0

This book is published by Jennifer Bell in conjunction with **WRITERSWORLD**, and is produced entirely in the UK. It is available to order from most bookshops in the United Kingdom, and is also globally available via UK based Internet book retailers.

WRITERSWORLD
2 Bear Close Flats, Bear Close, Woodstock
Oxfordshire, OX20 1JX, England
☎ 01993 812500
☎ +44 1993 812500
www.writersworld.co.uk

The text pages of this book are produced via an independent certification process that ensures the trees from which the paper is produced come from well managed sources that exclude the risk of using illegally logged timber while leaving options to use post-consumer recycled paper as well.

To M – my rock

Chapter 1

The Search

The train gathered pace, leaving M, my husband, on the sloping end of the platform, bent slightly forward, hands spread on thighs, trying to catch his breath.

I looked around the carriage, one of the old type that seated eight people at a push, with a door onto the corridor. All eyes were on me, shock and surprise on every face. One woman held the baby and another, Tim, the four year old. Our suitcase was on the floor. I clutched the pushchair, thrown in by M as he ran out of platform, pursued by the shouting guard. But we had done it. Nearly five years of searching and saving and we had, at last, found the country cottage, barn and acre of ground where we planned to start a pottery.

It had all begun after a holiday in Cornwall. Married two years, we had stayed in an ancient farmhouse deep in the west of the county. The magic of Cornwall had got to us. Why live a dreary nine to five existence in a city when there was an alternative?

Returning to London and our small flat on a busy crossroads, the plan took shape. We would sell the flat, send the furniture down to the Pickfords store in Penzance and return to Cornwall. Once there we could easily support ourselves, M had studied music at the Royal College of Music and pottery at art school in Oxford so was equipped to teach. I was a nurse and knew that I could find work anywhere. Decision made, we felt giddy with excitement, like children before a birthday party. We couldn't wait.

We left London on 14th April 1966. Snow had been forecast but, so late in the year, we didn't expect much. By Bagshott, no motorways in those days it was the A30 all the way, the scene was totally white with abandoned cars on either side. The road ran through silent pine woods, the only sounds the swish of the windscreen wipers and the squeak of fresh snow under the tyres. We made slow progress. An AA man in bright yellow stepped out, knocking snow off his heavy gauntlets and flagged us down.

"I advise you to give up," he said sternly, "conditions are terrible and the roads virtually impassable. It would be unwise to continue."

Thick flakes swirled around us as we considered.

We had an old Triumph Renown, a heavy car which gave good grip. The wipers, essential in this weather, could be manipulated from inside if necessary. We liked a challenge and were expected that night by a landlady in St. Austell. Besides, we had nothing to go back to. We carried on.

The snowy conditions continued well into the West Country and, although the roads were almost deserted, the journey took many hours more than normal. The mechanism of the windscreen wipers had given up with the weight of snow but, by turning the knob on the dashboard, with my arm threaded through the steering wheel, we were able to continue. We arrived supperless in the late evening to a cold welcome. A sharp, "Where have you been? I expected you hours ago," in an unheated B & B.

We sat on the edge of the double bed in the cheerless room and looked at each other. I nursed my right arm which had lost all feeling.

What had we done?

The next morning the sun shone in a clear blue Cornish sky and our spirits lifted. We drove into Fowey and explored its steep hills and narrow lanes, marvelling at the magnificent harbour and the view of the sea.

By the end of the day M had found a job as a milkman and I had met a rather exotic restaurateur who had taken me on as a waitress. The local grapevine mentioned a lone, tumbled caravan in a rutted field on a nearby farm and we settled ourselves in for the summer.

Sitting on the step of the caravan one evening, eating fried mackerel and crusty bread, we watched as the dusk crept from the hedgerows and a barn owl flew low, searching for his supper.

It was a beginning.

Summer was running out and I was pregnant – a baby and a winter in a damp caravan wouldn't be ideal. The time had come to be sensible again so M went to visit the Education Department at County Hall.

Two Cornish schools didn't have much in the way of music so he was asked to set up music departments, spending three days at Liskeard Grammar School and two at Callington. We knew that we couldn't afford the sort of property we really wanted: the cottage with the outbuildings which could eventually be turned into a pottery, so we settled for a bungalow in Looe which had a pretty garden and the sea at the end of the lane. Always in our minds was the thought that it would sell quickly, should we ever find and be able to afford our dream property.

M started teaching, Tim was born and every Friday M checked the estate agents in Liskeard for their coded drawing pins on a large map in reception. A green pin meant a country cottage.

We bought Ordinance Survey maps and trailed down dead end lanes at weekends, asking at farms for any unused or derelict property. We were prepared to take on anything but found nothing that we could afford. In those days mortgage companies were reluctant to lend on old property, particularly if renovation was needed, and usually demanded a 50% deposit.

Our second son, Mark, arrived. Looe was a pleasant place to live with small children. There was an energetic group of young mums: we looked after each other's children, played with them on the beach and eventually, raising money through grants and coffee mornings, started a playgroup.

It was the last afternoon of the summer term. The next day, the boys and I were catching the midday train from Plymouth. We were going to stay with my parents for a couple of weeks whilst M was away at an army camp. He made his usual call at the agents, just as the secretary was pushing a green pin into the board.

"Where's that cottage?" he asked.

"Out at Rosecraddoc, ten minutes from here, on the B road to Upton Cross. It's unoccupied at the moment," she added, "the owners have moved on."

M dashed off. As soon as he turned through the open gate and drew up, he knew.

It was a classic Cornish cottage, stone built, slate roofed, a linhay at one end and a barn at the other, together with an acre of land. He'd found it, and the price was right... just about.

With the car packed, we arrived at the agents first thing the next morning ready to put down a deposit. The previous evening, we'd phoned a broker we had got to know during our long search, given him the few details we had and asked him to fix us up with a mortgage while we were away.

The young agent, Peter Hooper, on duty that morning and handling his first sale, was shocked that we wanted to buy a house without seeing the inside and without me even seeing the outside. He said that this must be done. We followed him over there and he showed us in.

Worn slate floors, a huge granite fireplace, window seats within thick walls, an old range in the kitchen and, above everything, the sweet smell of it all. We were totally captivated but there was a train to catch.

We raced into Plymouth through the meandering Saturday traffic, abandoned the car and reached the platform, just as the guard raised his flag.

"We can't," I puffed, Tim on my shoulder.

"'We can," shouted my husband, already hauling a door open and unbuckling the baby.

And suddenly there we were – apologies all round, the shock and surprise turned to smiles and our luggage was stowed and seats found.

We were on our way.

Chapter 2

Beginnings

The cottage was perfect, sheltered by a hill behind with a sloping lawn in front, running into woodland. It was probably built in the eighteenth century but might well have been on older foundations. The Manor of Rosecraddoc was mentioned in the Domesday Book. The estate had been inherited by a Devon clergyman in the early 1800s and he had given the house a Georgian frontage, landscaped grounds and a tranquil lake to improve his view.

Our cottage had been the gardener's. It was the sort of place where, when you arrived, you would sit for a moment, breathing the silence before releasing a deep sigh of contentment. It got to most people. I watched visitors experiencing this tranquillity and even my down-to-earth, scientist father remarked, "I love arriving at Rosecraddoc. It has such a quality of peace."

Life continued. The children grew and started at the village school. I loved walking them home in the early dusk of a winter afternoon, and preparing their tea to the cawing of rooks in the tall tree that stood close to the kitchen.

We borrowed a billy goat to eat the overgrown grass and brambles in the orchard, M built a pig sty and we acquired a dozen plump brown hens. Our peace was only disturbed sometimes in the early hours. The first time, at the sound of heavy footsteps on the gravel, we awoke with a start, clutching each other in alarm. M went to the window and a drift of tobacco wafted through.

"'Only the milkman," came the call. It was 3am. Thereafter it was rather comforting to wake and smell his pipe before turning over and settling back into sleep.

M's music departments at the two schools flourished. Each developed a choir and an orchestra and more and more pupils took music as an exam subject. Eventually, the Liskeard post was made full-time.

We were visiting his brother and family who lived just outside Oxford when the accident happened. Again there had been a heavy snowfall and we had all taken toboggans into the sloping field opposite their house. Other family groups were there, the children bright spots of colour against the white snow. M started down the slope with Tim in front. The toboggan gathered speed, M stretched his leg out to slow down and there was a sudden sharp crack as his foot snagged in a rabbit hole. It was a bad break and a week in the Radcliffe Infirmary followed. Then the slow journey home to Cornwall.

Encased in plaster from hip to foot M was given a term's leave from teaching.

"'Don't think you're going to sit around doing nothing for three months," I said to him over breakfast one morning as he lavished a thick layer of marmalade onto his toast. My husband is very partial to marmalade and particular too. If it isn't homemade it has to be Frank Cooper's.

"You could use this time to get some designs going with the butter moulds." In the outbuilding attached to our cottage we had found three wood-wormy butter moulds. The designs and workmanship were fascinating. Made of finely grained wood, usually beech or sycamore, every farm had its own design which was stamped on the butter before being sold in the market. A readily identifiable trademark and a form of early advertising.

On our three moulds we had a formal swan design, an unusual acorn and a fairly common rose and thistle. We wondered how to turn these to practical use. Previously, we had made clay plaques with images of wild flowers. These were mounted on hessian and framed in pine. I sold them to shops quite easily but they were slow to sell to the public. Talking to buyers about reasons for this, I learnt the fairly obvious lesson that objects that have a practical use sell more readily than designs that hang on walls.

We had also, during the time spent looking for cottage premises, researched the different sorts of potteries. They seemed to fall into three categories:

1   Potteries, usually in tourist hot spots which made and sold directly to the public.
2   Studio potteries where the artist hand threw one-off designs and experimented with unusual glazes, exhibiting in galleries and at exhibitions.
3   Commercial potteries which produced a regular range of designs and sold to shops and stores.

We were reluctant to have the first sort of pottery which seemed to be a bit of a treadmill, churning out repetitive objects, mugs mostly, during the best part of the year in the summer season with lean times in the winter.

Studio pottery took time to establish and there was no certainty of success.

Commercial pottery seemed to be the most stable, promising regular hours and income. We just needed the right product, so we looked for a gap in the market.

During our research, we had contacted a firm in Bodmin who were the main suppliers of raw material.

"'However do you think you're going to make a living out of pottery?" they scoffed. "Don't you know there are already over 350 potteries in the West Country?"

We had to be different.

At that time, there seemed to be a gap in the market for good quality gifts, made in Britain. Our path became clearer. We would use the butter mould designs as lids for small containers which we would gift-box, designing the boxes so that the lids flipped up, making an instant display. To give added interest we would put a short history of butter moulds on one side. Boxes should also prove popular with buyers as they stacked easily in stock rooms and attractive packaging added to their appeal for customers looking for presents.

Propped up against the wheel in our draughty barn with the lower part of his broken leg encased in a plastic bag, M started work producing containers and painstakingly pressing lids.

We needed a drying cupboard so bought a large double-fronted wardrobe at the local auction house. M lined each side with shelving made from hardboard with holes in it and installed a greenhouse heater underneath. It worked beautifully, the pots drying slowly and evenly over a couple of days until they were ready for the kiln.

Now we had to find a box maker. I tried local companies first with little success. The problem was always in committing ourselves to a large enough run for the work to be commercially viable for the box company. None were interested in the seed corn point of view. In fact, a large company in Plymouth told me, rather patronisingly, to run away and return when we could order in hundreds. Useless to plead that if we couldn't afford to start, we would never reach that sort of size. I was more than a little irked by the owner's manner and took some pleasure several years later when we were approached by his company, touting for our business. I said that our excellent box company had been good enough to support us in the beginning and that we had no intention of changing supplier.

I eventually made contact with a company in Yeovil through their West Country agent which agreed to help and make an initial small run of gift boxes in three sizes.

It was now spring – Easter was approaching, the start of the holiday season and we needed to do some selling. Thinking that with the country theme of our designs, the National Trust would be a good place to start, I rang Killerton, then the headquarters for the National Trust in the South West and asked to speak to the person in charge of sales. I was put through to a pleasant sounding gentleman with a rich tweedy voice and an appointment was made.

M said that he was coming too. Understandable that he wanted to be included in the fun after all his hard work but tricky as, with his inflexible full-length plaster, he had to be fitted into our small car. Eventually we discovered that if he sat in the middle of the back seat, his plastered leg could be lifted over the passenger seat and threaded through the gap over the gear lever. This was great for him as he was able to enjoy his first outing for weeks, but driving was awkward, especially changing gear and I seem to remember that we did a lot of that one and a half hour journey in second.

I cringe when I remember the naivety of my presentation, with the six pots, sitting on hay in a shallow flower basket. There wasn't much talking. The buyer, whose name I discovered was Warren Davies, handled each pot slowly, carefully removing and replacing each lid, inspecting the base (a mental note for me – should we be thinking of a trademark?) and sitting each pot in turn, in a line, on his polished mahogany desk.

He sat staring at them for several minutes, deep in thought. Tension rising, eventually I could take no more. Clearing my throat nervously, I ventured, "Do you think that this is the sort of thing the National Trust might be interested in?"

"Oh yes, oh yes, most definitely so," came his positive response. "I'm going to write you orders for each of our outlets in the South West and we would like them in for Easter."

Cripes! Thanking him and collecting the pots and as many wisps of hay from his desk as I could manage, I walked quietly back through the two offices and across the car park, exuberation bubbling beneath the surface.

Pots stowed, I sat back in the driving seat.

"Well?" from my husband.

"Orders for every outlet."

"How many is that?"

"I've no idea," passing him the paperwork, "but they want them for Easter."

Our excitement was quickly replaced by trepidation. How on earth were we to do it? Back home we counted the numbers, divided by the days left, leaving a few on the end for deliveries and made out the rota. Sixty pots a day may not sound much but all had to be done by hand. Made, dried, fettled[1], biscuit-fired, glazed and finally fired again. Disasters, mainly occurring in the firing processes, had to be allowed for.

A strict regime began, the day divided into children, food,

---

[1] Fettle – to trim or smooth the rough edge of a pot before firing.

essential chores, pared to a minimum, dust didn't count, then pots. Trays of pots in various stages of preparation began to take up floor space, first in the old cobbled dairy and then throughout the house. The heedless stampede of children, home from school or in from the garden, prompted shouts of, "Slowly, slowly, mind the pots!"

The promised boxes didn't arrive. My phone calls became increasingly frantic. Each deadline passed. Still nothing. Tim and Mark were having their tea at the kitchen table. Time was very short. We couldn't wait or accept promises any longer. Telling the boys to keep quiet as I had an important phone call to make, I picked up the receiver.

"The boxes should have been here three weeks ago."

"You have broken several promises."

"There are only three days now to our deadline when orders have to be delivered."

"Are you trying to ruin our business before it has even got started?" and so on...

A bit of a verbal onslaught which left Tim and Mark open mouthed.

"Mum, we've never heard you like that before."

"Well," I smiled, "now you have, you know not to push me!"

The call had ended with a promise, firm this time I hoped, that the work would be finished immediately and the boxes Red Starred on British Rail to Plymouth on Friday. Friday! That was Good Friday the day that orders were due in the shops.

The boys, pots and M were piled into the car, M now thankfully in a shorter plaster. We met the train and, wheeling a trolley along the platform, was the guard with our Red Starred parcels.

The day was sunny, a beautifully calm Good Friday. We took everything up to The Hoe and started packing pots to a stirring performance of The St. Matthew Passion broadcast on Radio 3. The boys lolled against the sea wall and licked ice creams while we worked. A touting fisherman asked if we'd like to take a trip across to Drake Island.

"Go away!" came simultaneously from both of us.

The last order of a very long day was delivered in the late evening.

Never was fish and chips enjoyed so much on the way home!

Chapter 3

Growing

The summer progressed and the pots sold well. Our mad routine continued – even harder now that M's leg was healed and he was back at school. Teaching music meant that evenings were often busy with choir and orchestra practices. Cramming our pottery production into the remaining space meant that there was sometimes no time even to answer the telephone.

Several things became apparent: hand making was no longer possible, we needed a machine. If we bought a machine we could make more. We needed help and we would need more outlets and, eventually, more working space. We had heard of a machine, much used in the Potteries, that group of historic towns whose names are redolent of the history of English pottery and porcelain, called a jig and jolley (that name somehow always reminds me of Morris dancing). It's essentially a wheel which takes a mould, speeding production and guaranteeing constant sizes. It was exciting to think of having such a machine and its possibilities. We put an advert in a newspaper which circulated in the five towns and were contacted by a firm, in Burslem, which had a second-hand machine to sell. These machines are incredibly awkward to move and very heavy so, the money sorted, we hired a large van and two, solid-looking men who drove up to collect it.

Arriving late at night with the factory closed, they decided to sleep in the van and load the jig and jolley first thing in the morning. They were woken by police sirens, barking dogs and finally the doors of the van were wrenched open and a glaring light shone in on them. In their bemused state, they couldn't work out what was happening but, with IRA activity at its height, they eventually discovered that a neighbour in the street of terraced houses had reported a suspicious vehicle and the police had arrived speedily to investigate.

We started farming out a lot of the fettling work to Ruth, a neighbour who became a great friend. An arts graduate, Ruth had come down to Cornwall during the war as a land girl and married Wes, a farm worker. Wes, short for Wesley – the Methodist tradition remains strong in Cornwall – had a passion for steam engines and was building a working model, having first made his own lathe. We would sometimes meet him in the lanes, leaning on a gate, gazing at the horizon.

"Stretching his eyes," he called it.

Robert, their last child of five, was a little older than Tim and they became good friends. Rob would run down to us in the mornings for a lift along the lanes to school a couple of miles away and Tim and he would walk home together, often tickling trout in the little stream that ran alongside the lane. They lifted one so frequently from his basking position on a sandy bank that they did it sometimes on request for tourists.

The two boys were also up for adventure. The telephone rang one night, its shrill tone penetrating our dreams. A ringing phone in the night is rarely good news; M was already reaching for it. I waited, my heart pounding.

I could hear the loud, authoritative voice.

"Do you have a son called Timothy?"

"Yes," M was puzzled.

"Where is he?"

"In bed."

"You might like to check on that sir."

M padded across the landing and came back swiftly.

"His bed is empty."

"We have him here sir," a pause, "in the police station at Launceston." And then sternly, "Please come and collect him and his friend – as soon as possible."

Muttering to himself M dressed quickly, grabbed the car keys and left.

Tim and Rob had decided to go off on a night-time bike ride. Rob, with the only alarm clock, set it for 2am, Tim tied a piece of string to his big toe and dangled the end out of the window for Rob to tug. They set off through the lanes for Launceston but were picked up a few miles short by a police patrol car.

Tim was thoroughly ticked off by both the police sergeant and by us but we certainly admired his spirit.

So, Ruth fettled trays of pots at home, along with another

17

couple of outworkers we had taken on, and came to the pottery a couple of afternoons a week to catch up with the glazing.

Now that production was on a sounder foundation we needed more outlets.

My maternal grandparents had lived in Snowdonia whilst we were growing up. It was bliss to spend time with them, to have the freedom of the woods and the mountain which rose behind the house and they'd taught me a great deal.

Grandpa was a quiet, modest man with such a dry sense of humour that, sometimes, people at the dinner table, getting the joke rather late, would chortle suddenly, long after the conversation had moved on. One piece of advice that I remember vividly, said seriously but with his usual light-hearted twinkle, "If you ever want to do anything in life, always start at the top. It's quicker."

I thought of London and my favourite shops. Where would our pots fit in and which shop's name would carry weight with other prospective buyers? I had always loved Liberty's. It was my first destination on a shopping trip. I loved the atmosphere of the Tudor-style buildings and wandering amongst the fabrics, the antiques and the amazing richness of the Oriental carpets.

Taking a deep breath, I picked up the telephone and rang the Liberty number.

"Could I speak to the buyer please, the buyer for your gift department."

"That'll be Mr. Andrews. Who shall I say is calling?"

"He won't know me, I'm ringing from Cornwall and I'd like to make an appointment to come and see him."

"Just one moment please." So much nicer than the 'bear with me' that you get today.

Then, magically, Mr. Andrews, who very kindly agreed to see me.

A trip to London on the train. A rare treat but a lot to be organised first.

Boys, meals, animals and pottery work sorted out and

remembering to take M's school telephone number with me, on a piece of paper in my purse, no mobiles in those days, I caught the early express to London. What bliss. Four hours with nothing to do but read the paper, have a coffee and dream out of the window at the passing landscape, until the tacky London suburbs reached out to engulf us. Then the enormous bustling noise of Paddington, a few stops on the Underground, the curving stately buildings of Regent Street and Liberty's. I entered the lovely old building, threw a brief glance at the tantalising displays of scarves and accessories, then mounted the oak staircase to Mr. Andrews' office.

The, by now standard, formula, a handshake and a, 'thank you for seeing me' while I opened my new, professional-looking case of designs. Again, the buyer looked at each pot carefully, testing lids and turning each pot upside down – we really must decide on a trademark. I scarcely breathed. So much of our fledgling business depended on this order. Although there were plenty of good department stores in London, thinking and aiming for it over the months, Liberty's had become a sort of talisman in my mind. If they said yes nothing was beyond us. A short time later, having answered the usual questions, mostly about methods of manufacture, reliability and production times, Mr. Andrews may, from my answers, have imagined that we were a rather larger business that the kitchen table affair of reality. We exchanged smiles and handshakes again and I sped up the stairs, threading my way through clustered shoppers with as much decorum as I could manage, to the public telephone on the antiques floor.

The school secretary answered.

"Could you get a message to M for me Jude?"

"Of course. What is it?"

"Just say Liberty's say yes."

I bought a sandwich and sat on a bench in Hyde Park, listened to the singing birds amongst the summer flowers, savouring the moment before the long journey back to Cornwall.

Chapter 4

Publicity/Design Council/Harrogate

Events moved swiftly after that. Once the pots reached Liberty's, they were seen by Lucia van der Post who had a Saturday column in the *Financial Times*. Her article resulted in a contact from the Design Council, then in the Haymarket. The D.C., together with its shop, the Design Centre, was an enormously useful institution for small businesses. Run by a board of people prominent in the design world, its remit was to encourage good business designs and it awarded a coveted black and white label to producers who met Design Council standards.

This label, on our boxes, created great cachet for the product and gave buyers, particularly those from other countries (the Americans loved it) confidence to order. Another bonus was in making it much easier to attend foreign trade fairs. The Design Centre would make a block booking of 20-30 stands and we would all exhibit together in a highly visible space under the British flag. An official from the commercial department of the embassy or consulate would also be present who would answer questions on export procedure and foreign tariffs. I grew to love the meetings which preceded an overseas foray; so focussed and lively, especially compared with the turgid proceedings at N.H.S. meetings I had observed as a nurse. A group of bright, sparky small business owners would convene around the board table. Ideas exchanged, plans presented, discussed, decisions made, all in an hour or so before dispersing back to more important work – but – these foreign trade shows were all in the future.

It was coming up to Christmas, orders were rapidly accumulating and we needed help again.

There was a farm next door, its old orchard adjoined ours; a tangle of grass, brambles and spreading blossom in the spring. I had once watched a 'parliament' of rooks there, an event steeped in country lore. The birds, there must have been over thirty, sat in a loose circle all twittering together for several minutes before suddenly flying off in different directions.

Bill, who worked on this farm, known as Oliver's, had a nice wife. I knew that she wasn't working and, with four children, thought she might be glad of some extra money coming up to Christmas. She agreed to help us over the busy period – none of us knowing that ten years later she would still be there.

She proved to be an enormous asset. Talented and full of common sense she took to the work like a natural. Her name was Joyce, or rather that was what we called her for a long time, probably at least for a couple of years, until one day an insurance agent called, and asked if he could speak to Sandra, who, he had been told, worked at the pottery. I was puzzled.

"We don't have a Sandra here."

Her voice from the barn interrupted.

"Yes we do. That's me." Later on I asked, "Is your name Sandra?"

"Yes," she said.

"Then why have we been calling you Joyce all this time?"

"I've no idea," she laughed, "but I prefer it to Sandra so I've never put you right."

With a more stable work force who could keep the pottery running whilst we were away, we decided to do our first trade show.

The idea of having a stand where buyers came to us was infinitely preferable to visiting individual shops in strange towns in other parts of the country, which had been our main selling method so far.

I loathed the time spent in, first, finding a suitable shop (traffic wardens were always a good source of information), then going in cold and asking to speak to the proprietor. The knowing and sometimes pitying look from an assistant who had seen so many disappointed sellers before. Then the silent period when the owner would contemplate the array of pots and I would wait, wondering anxiously, for a decision. Later, I was told by an agent that with cold calls, one was lucky to get a success rate of one in twenty. We did rather better than that but it was a stressful experience and I was stupidly often glad when we arrived in a town to find that it was early closing!

Harrogate was to be our first trade show. Another organisation at that time which helped small businesses was CoSira: Council for Small Industries in Rural Areas. Ted Mahoney came to see us. He suggested that my tottering piles of paperwork could be better organised and helpfully showed me how to write a balance sheet, solving a worry that had been at the back of my mind for some time. I had heard of 'cash flow', a common enough term now but not much heard of in those days. I wasn't sure what it was and was afraid that I'd missed something significant. Discovering that it was simply the inflow of money compared to the outgoings came as a great relief and another niggle that disturbed sleep from time to time vanished.

Following Ted's visit, we advertised for secretarial help, preferably someone who was versatile and wouldn't mind also helping out in the pottery.

Chris breezed in with all the vigour of a fresh wind from across the Atlantic. A Canadian, from Toronto, she had grown up in her own family's small business so she knew how things should work. She tackled my stacks of paper, ignoring my plaintive, "But I know where that is Chris – about three inches down on the second pile," and we soon had neat files on a shelving system in the old hay store, now designated as our office.

She worked rapidly and efficiently when called into the pottery and even washed, unasked, my kitchen floor once when I was particularly harassed and expecting visitors.

It was May when we set off for Harrogate, blossom and cowslips lining the roads as we progressed north. We negotiated the contrary traffic of Leeds – always hard to get right first time and drove into the delights of the grey-stoned buildings and floral displays of Harrogate.

We claimed our small space, rather nervously, everyone else looked so professional, so confident, arranged our pots on the hessian covered table and hung a large poster we had had made of the cottage and pottery as a back-drop. Ted Mahoney passed on his rounds and cheered us by making encouraging noises.

Our pots sold steadily, backed by the confidence given by the names of our existing stockists: The National Trust, Liberty's and the Design Centre.

One poignant little episode happened on our first day, a Sunday, the day when family shops are able to visit. We discovered subsequently that Sundays are always chaotic with family parties, often of three generations, crowding the aisles and, from a business point of view, the orders are small and not particularly exciting.

I noticed a small child of about four, wandering in our aisle, apparently on his own. He was lost so he and I set off for the office. On the way I explained that he wasn't to worry, that the woman in the office would put out a message over the loud speakers and his parents would come and collect him.

He looked at me sideways, a serious and solid little boy.

"I am quite worried really," he said in his flat, Yorkshire voice. "You see, they've got a new baby at 'ome and I'm afraid that they might not come back for me."

It nearly broke my heart and I hope I reassured him that, however tired and short of time parents are with a new baby, no one is ever as special as the first one and, I was sure, his parents would be searching for him anxiously.

That smallish craft fair in Harrogate was a good place to learn the ropes. We made friends amongst the other small businesses – cross-fertilization is always useful and we enjoyed convivial evenings at an Italian restaurant in the town.

Home again and enjoying an enticing spell of early summer sunshine, I rang Ruth.

"I've got an appointment up on the north coast tomorrow. D'you want to come? I thought we could set off early and take a picnic... find a spot on the cliffs."

"Done," from Ruth, "and I'll make the pasties for lunch."

Ruth's pasties were the best. Definitely the best in Cornwall, possibly the best ever made, anywhere.

She had two secrets. The pastry had to be made from

dripping. Not any old shop-bought dripping, but homemade, full of flavour with meaty bits. Then, to each little pile of swede, potato and beef on its circle of pastry, she would add a good dollop of butter. The result was a deliciously succulent pasty, quite the best food to enjoy sitting amid the wild pinks and springing turf of a sunny cliff top, watching the long Atlantic rollers breaking on the rocks below.

Chapter 5

Trade Shows/Unions/Danielle

The following year, encouraged by the Harrogate experience, we decided to tackle the Birmingham Gift Fair held in March in the National Exhibition Centre. This was the largest and most exciting event of its kind in the country. Just to arrive, to see the vast car parks, the railway station, to hear the roar of approaching aircraft landing nearby, then the row of flags and line of diplomatic cars...

There were five huge halls and, if you had a good product, orders were virtually guaranteed and could be from anywhere in the world. Held over five days, it was certainly stimulating, if exhausting, and reduced your voice to a whisper for some time afterwards.

But, it was a very difficult show to break into. We were advised to go on a waiting list and take anything offered in Hall 5, the place for small businesses.

Luck was on our side and, a couple of weeks before the show, we were contacted by Wendy, a graphic designer who was looking for someone to share both the space and the cost of her stand. We agreed immediately and together designed a layout which gave us each a display space and a centre table and chairs where, we hoped, buyers would write their orders. A jar of curving yellow tulips decorated this table.

By this time, we had a representative, Ray White, ex-army, confident and charming. An experienced salesman he had taken on selling for us in London and the Home Counties.

Wendy was a sweet girl but excessively protective of her beautifully designed range of paper ware, inverting the usual selling process by giving each prospective buyer a grilling regarding the suitability of their premises for her product. Ray, helping on our stand one morning, observed this technique used on a buyer for a well-known chain and, seeing the order placed in jeopardy, he caught M's eye, took a tulip out of the vase and ate it.

Birmingham over the years became a valuable venue for us, a good source of orders and contacts but there was one big drawback. The unions at this time during the late 1970s were very powerful. Their diktats had to be obeyed or your stand would be blacked out. I have seen exhibitors reduced to tears when either an item of electrical equipment, perfectly acceptable in the outside world, or a piece of their display met with union displeasure and all had to be changed, sometimes at great cost.

By this particular year we had worked our way into the central aisle, not too near the start; we had noticed that buyers only began paying attention after the first half dozen or so stands. We always booked the same sized space which all our display units were made to fit and I had only given the floor plan a cursory glance after our cheque had gone through.

The car was playing up. Usually it was completely reliable but there was a problem with the steering and had been for quite some time. It had been checked by two garages and no fault discovered but still M wasn't happy. He wouldn't allow me to drive as he felt he had to be ready for a sudden emergency. An added strain on an already tiring day.

We were glad to reach the N.E.C. safely.

We paid our deposit and were given our time slot. Only half an hour for unloading, then the car had to be moved to a more distant car park. We reached our stand, M manoeuvring the laden trolley through the littered aisles, while I balanced a swaying pile of paperwork and stopped, amazed – the stand was double the size ordered. Later we discovered that a last minute cancellation had included that space in ours. Of course we had nowhere near enough material with us to furnish this larger stand. Never mind. We found the furniture depot where you could hire extra equipment and breathed a sigh of relief. With a table, chairs and carpeting, we could spread the pottery display around and it would still look acceptable.

There was a problem. The unions have closed their lists now, we were told, and won't fit the carpet squares.

"That's all right," we responded cheerfully, "we can do that for ourselves."

"Oh no you won't. The unions won't allow it. They'll black your stand."

"But what are we to do?"

"Sorry we can't help."

And no amount of explanation and pleading would change their minds.

We returned to our space and poured a cup of coffee. 7pm. Everywhere was jostling activity, pictures, fabrics, stationary, ceramics, all the paraphernalia of setting up a stand crowded the floor. Heavy union men with bulging tool belts finishing off their last jobs. Industrial cleaners standing by. Attendants with huge rolls of carpets, ready to roll the minute an aisle was clean. Our space looked bleaker by the minute as other stands took shape.

"There's nothing for it," said M eventually. "We'll have to go back to Cornwall and collect more stuff ourselves."

"But what about the car?"

"We'll just have to risk it."

We made it home in four hours. Packed the car with more rush matting taken from our office, a garden table and folding chairs, a large jug and daffodils picked by torch light from the garden and a pile of empty gift boxes to add to the display.

Two hours rest and we set off again.

A little way into the journey we met fog which thickened through the Midlands. Time passed very slowly. We travelled silently and tensely, other traffic just faint shapes in the mist. M's hands were tight on the steering wheel, ready for trouble. At last the N.E.C. loomed, the car parks deserted, just the harsh, greenish glare of overhead lights.

We were still working on the stand ten minutes before opening when a group of suited officials paused and one remarked sarcastically,

"Some people do leave it to the last minute."

It wasn't worth replying.

The doors opened. The public flooded in. We felt shaky with cotton-wool legs and eyes gritty like sandpaper. Still, our stressful story had spread amongst friends on other stands and we definitely benefitted with a sympathy vote from buyers. It was good to leave at the end of a long day with the prospect of a quick supper and bed.

At trade shows we had always followed the rule that, however quiet the day, we would never leave early, so we would watch the stream of exhibiters, paperwork tucked under arms, girls wobbling, Dick Emery-like on high heels and long to be off too but we always stuck it out, just in case. This paid off once where an overseas buyer rushed back, just on closing, and gave us a huge order which made the entire show more than worthwhile.

This provoked M to leave a message for a friend who had left early as usual. He sold stationary.

M's message read: "Five fifty. Where are you? W.H. Smith?"

Our friend arrived in the morning, saw the message and looked shocked until he turned and saw M smiling...

M's jokes were not always appreciated by me. I feared losing orders when he, a keen follower of Test Match cricket, pinned a card on our stand, "To all Australians. You Lost."

Trade shows weren't just about taking orders, it was always worth talking to visitors who had paused to look at the stand. One encounter with an American went:

"Is this your sort of product? Would you like to see a catalogue?"

A southern drawl. "No, not really. My line is barbeque equipment back in the United States."

"Could we do anything for you? We can make special orders to your design."

It turned out that he had always wanted terracotta lanterns to add to his range. That evening we worked out a few ideas over supper. I loved doing this. M was always practical and reined in my wilder flights. He also had a very good eye for design on the 'less is more' principle. The Texan returned the next morning, approved the design and orders followed.

It was also always worthwhile getting a card from people and contacting them a few weeks after a show when everything had settled down.

Once, a Swiss buyer, who worked as an agent for several

companies, had just been asked to find an appropriate container to sell alongside Alpine products. Our 'cow' design fitted the bill and ongoing orders were the result.

We loved the excitement and the stimulation that came from these encounters although there was one which M was not keen to follow through.

Danielle was from Hong Kong. A lawyer's daughter, at sixteen she had left her home, flown to France and presented herself at the Pierre Cardin Studio in Paris. She modelled for him for several years but had now set up a business selling gift products, made to her own design.

She wanted us to make large bowls, mixing bowl size. No problems there but our kilns would only take six or so at a time which meant either increasing the price ridiculously or reducing the profit. Not an appealing proposition when we could sell all we made of our own range. Usually, the more pots packed into a kiln, the greater the profit so we had never been keen to make large objects.

Our most profitable line had come about by accident. One of our earliest designs was an individual butter pat container with a lid. Despite having the jig and jolley moulds so that size was constant, variable shrinkage during firing, depending on the pot's position in the kiln, meant that we always had to make more bases than lids to ensure pairing, and these bases had begun to pile up. I had the sudden thought one day that, if we could make a functioning butter mould, we might be able to use these extra bases. Experiments followed; the little pots were filled with butter and hardened in the fridge, the small butter mould was soaked in cold water then inverted and the design impressed on the butter. It worked!

We packed this new product, four butter pots in a long box with a working butter mould in the centre and sent it off to the Design Council. Approval followed, plus the coveted D.C. label. These butter mould sets sold really well and became one of the mainstays of our range.

Back to Danielle. She was determined to get her large glazed bowls and pursued M relentlessly at all trade shows. By this time, in addition to Harrogate and the N.E.C., we did two Top Drawer shows in Kensington and the Spring Fair in Torquay. This latter, the first of the year held in January, was easy as it was close to home and was a good rehearsal for the N.E.C. in Birmingham.

M kept refusing to produce Danielle's pots and used every excuse he could think of: lack of space, extra time for firing, the expense – new equipment would be needed for the jig and jolley etc. etc. In the end she confronted him.

"If you did make them, how much would you have to charge?"

M made a face at me, then named a ridiculously over-the-top figure. Danielle's hand shot out, "Done!" she cried.

The initial order was for six. We thought that that would be that, as the whole design process was so complicated and expensive, and we continued normal production with relief.

To explain. The large pots were sent to Madeira to have individual wicker baskets fashioned around them, then up to Scotland where they were fitted with five wicks and filled with scented candle wax, the perfume coming from Helena Rubenstein in Paris.

Danielle rang us early one morning to say that she had taken the completed designs to Harvey Nichols in Knightsbridge and they had bought all six. The selling price was astronomical. Opinion in the pottery, in this tiny, unsophisticated hamlet on the edge of Bodmin Moor was that they would never sell until, maybe, the summer sales... maybe.

At coffee time the phone rang. It was Danielle.

"Harvey Nichols have just rung and they've sold all six to an Italian customer. They want another twelve!"

M put his head in his hands.

Rosecraddoc as we found it.

Cartoon by Gordon Metcalfe

M/Malcolm at work.

Jennifer, M, Tim, Mark.

Designs with a Difference

A unique range of terracotta pottery with a country look

The designs include a range of, "Savoury Food Pots", soup and cereal bowls, butter and biscuit moulds (all gift-boxed with recipes), wine coolers and kitchen accessories

Malcolm and Jennifer Bell

Rosecraddoc Pottery Liskeard Cornwall England
Telephone 0579 42883

Trade Stand

Mitzi.

Joyce and one of the Margarets.

Rosecraddoc Pottery as we left it.

Chapter 6

Plymouth Market/Expansion

We had already renovated the small space between house and barn where a cow had been milked on a cobbled floor, putting down a modern, concrete floor and using the cobbles to surface the little courtyard where we also had a dovecote with fluttering white doves, but the barn and this old dairy were not enough. Now we added a long extension on the far side of the barn which gave us a good production area and space for two, new, electric kilns. This new building extended forwards, making an 'L' shape with the barn and the extra space, became a small gift shop and a store for finished products.

The electric kilns were put on overnight tariff which obviously gave us cheaper electricity but meant that M had to switch on in the evenings. Then a couple of times a week for a biscuit firing, had to get up in the early hours to throw the last switch. This chore had its upside for my generally anti-social husband. It gave him the perfect get-out from attending certain events, he had to, "Switch a kiln on."

Rob, now sixteen, had left his boarding school in North Cornwall and come to us full time. He had already been very useful doing pocket-money work in the holidays. Always steady and reliable, we appreciated his practical skills and his slow, dry sense of humour. His father's steam engine, after two or three years' painstaking work, was nearing completion and had reached a critical phase. One morning, a certain tricky process was make or break. Rob went off for lunch and we waited.

The door opened. "Well?" from M.

"No good. It broke."

"What did your father say?"

Rob stared at the floor – a long, thoughtful pause.

"Well it wasn't tut, tut, deary me."

This became something of a catch phrase in the pottery afterwards whenever a problem arose.

Tim and Mark were old enough to give a hand with the pottery work (for payment of course) and, especially during weekends, they would make sure their activities kept them near enough to hear the outside bell for the shop, where they were on ten percent, taking strict turns.

We sold seconds only, a good way of reducing the pile. Joyce was especially vigilant in keeping standards up and anything with the slightest flaw found its way to the baskets in the shop.

Every now and again, with these baskets filling up, M and I would set off early and take a pitch in the Plymouth outdoor market – now, sadly, a car park. We always enjoyed these ventures. Exciting to be amongst the professional marketeers and experience another style of selling.

We would arrive early with the vans and pantechnicons and, after setting up, queue for bacon butties and strong tea, then watch as seasoned traders opened their pink *Financial Times* and talked stocks and shares. It was all a bit of an eye-opener.

Customers could be tricky too. It was common for people to want perfect pots for seconds prices and then to demand a gift box, "As it's for a present."

One well-dressed woman, having sorted several items to her liking, then harangued M about their faults, ending with, "I know you market traders, always trying to pull a fast one."

"Madame," M replied, "I would very much rather you didn't buy anything than be unhappy." And he removed the pots from her hands. She changed her attitude rapidly and tried to take them back but M refused to sell her anything and, eventually, she had to retreat.

We were now packing orders in the restricted space of the gift shop and storing large numbers of gift boxes and packing materials on the 'industrial shelf' my father and M had built in the barn, using huge bolts plugged into the rat-holed, cob walls and accessed via a metal staircase.

My father had spent most of his working life with Unilever, latterly improving the efficiency of factory production lines. He tried very hard to bring the pottery up to his exacting standard but I'm afraid we sadly disappointed him – although I think he enjoyed very much being involved in our enterprise when he was staying in Cornwall.

Our different attitudes were summed up very early in the business when we were staying with my parents in Cheshire after a selling trip. We were relaxing one evening and talking about costing on these exercises.

My brother-in-law jumped in with, "Yes I know, you must be sure to cost in your petrol."

Father said, quite rightly, "Not only that but your time, wear and tear on the car, parking fees, accommodation etc."

M and I laughed and said that we knew that we should be doing these things but we regarded the trips as welcome breaks and treated them as a bit of a holiday.

Dad was sorely vexed by our flippancy – perhaps we shouldn't have teased him so much but his help, especially his mathematical skills, were invaluable. He was the only one in the family who could work out the shrinkage of new designs and tell us what size gift box to order.

We badly needed a packing room to store both gift boxes and outers: used, stout cardboard cartons that we collected from a local photographic company in exchange for contributions to their Christmas party/social fund.

We heard that a football team in Saltash was building a proper changing room and that their large, old wooden building was for sale. We went over to have a look and it seemed perfect – the right size, about 20'x12' and the wood in good condition. I'm a keen gardener and it was always with a pang of regret that another piece of garden had to be sacrificed but the building fitted in well. Our friendly builder put down a concrete base, polishing the concrete with a whirring disc to a finish worthy of a living room and a local farmer delivered the then flat-pack building on his tractor and trailer. We laid paving stones to join the building to the gift shop and covered the join with a glass roof on sturdy timber supports – a trip to the Duchy Nursery in Lostwithiel to find roses and clematis to grow up those posts finished the job.

Lined with steel shelving with space for bales of shredded paper, this building worked really well and it was a relief and a huge time saver to have all the elements for packing orders within very easy reach under one roof. It became a pleasant job and I enjoyed afternoons, peacefully assembling orders with the radio for company.

We had various methods of delivery. For the UK we had done a deal with a national carrier and they came and collected weekly. For most export orders we used shipping agents: enormously useful people who would take delivery at the docks, usually Felixstowe, a fairly new enterprise which had grown quickly during the container evolution and had established a reputation for efficiency and reliability. The agent at the docks would deal with all the paperwork, deliver to his opposite number in say, South Africa, where the shipment would be held at the docks until word was received from us that payment had been cleared.

For most of Europe, having experienced bad debts and the difficulties of chasing these in other countries, we had turned to the Post Office.

Cartons could be sent from the post office in Liskeard, our nearest town, and delivered throughout the continent, cash on delivery. Although we had to wait up to six months for our money to find its way back to us through the system, the method was fail-safe and satisfied both parties.

Taking these Europe-bound cartons into the Liskeard Post Office though was a bit of a nightmare. The boxes, often six at a time, were too heavy to carry far and there were only five parking spaces outside Webb's Hotel, next to the Post Office in the middle of town. I usually left the trip until late afternoon when it was quieter but even with a free space I could easily overrun the twenty minute time limit, especially as each carton needed five different forms, only possible to complete at the post office counter. I got to know Norman, the traffic warden, quite well and he was very understanding and tolerant. One day though, I emerged late, to find a parking ticket. Looking up I saw Norman rushing towards me. "You've changed the car," he accused. "I wouldn't have given you a ticket if I'd known it was yours."

After that episode and the hold-up to normal business whenever our orders appeared, a rep came to see me and we were able to set up a small post office on our own premises, the van calling on request.

During the warm days of summer the van doors would be left open whilst we completed paperwork and a couple of times Mitzi, our small, black and white cat, had to be chased out of the back where she had found a cosy bed on a sack of mail.

We lost Mitzi once; for about a fortnight and were quite frantic. We searched the woods where she sometimes walked with us, mewing when she'd had enough and wanted to be carried home. We asked all our neighbours if they'd seen her and pinned posters to gates and trees.

We gave up hope.

Then, one afternoon, I was working in the garden, when a shadow, slipping through the gate, caught my eye. It was Mitzi, limping, dusty and exhausted but home again. I picked her up carefully and carried her into the kitchen. She could hardly stand but drank a bowl of warm milk, all I dared give her, before collapsing into her basket in front of the Rayburn. She slept, with only a break to take food and quickly visit the garden, for about three days.

We guessed that she must have climbed into the post office van and travelled, probably to some outlying farm on Bodmin Moor.

We were so glad to have her home again.

Chapter 7

Recession/Recipes/U.S.A./Border Adventures

Recession bit sharply in the early eighties. Interest rates rose to 14% and inflation was around 20%. Raw materials and production costs were all going up fast, workers needed pay rises and the N.E.C. Spring Show in Birmingham was coming. We were terrified at the prospect of putting our prices up to cover all this but equally terrified at the thought of what would happen if we didn't. The responsibility for our workers, their wellbeing and that of their families, weighed on us.

I remember Joyce at the door of the shop as we set off, her anxious expression as she wished us luck. "You can only do your best, don't worry, I'm sure you'll be alright."

The previous year, as the economic outlook worsened, inflation rose and orders began to fall away; I had rung half a dozen of our best buyers and asked them what continued to sell during a recession. The answers, from all, were identical. Anything to do with children or food. This made sense. No one wants their children to suffer and parents will deny themselves to support their young but that didn't help us. Food, though, that was another matter.

We already made containers and had gift boxes which could easily be adapted to carry recipes.

A period of experiment followed. Not liking to copy from others, I devised, with the advice of an aunt, a Cordon Bleu cook who had taught at Constance Spry's school in Winkfield, a series of savoury recipes. Meeting the boys off the Plymouth train after school the conversation (if 'conversation' with teenage boys is the right word) would go, "What's for supper?"

The reply, "It's an experiment," would provoke general groans and rolling of eyes.

None the less, both Tim and Mark took a keen interest in the new recipes and gave considered opinions on my various offerings and each in his own way later became a very good cook.

One design which showed a dramatic improvement in sales after the recipe treatment was the soup bowl. This was a basic terracotta bowl with our traditional, dark brown interior glaze. It had a lid with a small knob and a crimped edge – the more esoteric shops called it a 'marmite pot'. How to make it stand out from all the other soup bowls on the market? We packed ours in twos, one above the other and had a hot winter soup recipe, with dumplings, on one side and a chilled summer one on the other. Called 'Soup for Two' it was an instant present and fell within the price range for birthday and engagement gifts.

We had also learnt that there were certain price bands that customers were willing to pay, with wedding presents being the most expensive. You had to work backwards, removing the VAT and retail mark-up before arriving at our selling price. Setting the final selling price always involved both, adding all our costings together, with a margin for profit and looking at it from the other end – what the market would bear.

We had learnt early that a successful business is always looking to decrease costs and increase profits. This could sound greedy and confirm the belief of anti-capitalists that businesses only want to make money, but actually, this apparently contradictory course results in a business which thrives, giving profit to both invest in new machinery and reward workers.

During this period we also acquired a part-time book keeper – a very large lady but always simply and stylishly dressed so that you weren't really aware of her size. She had a touch of the Hattie Jacques about her though, which terrified everyone, especially M when she was on the trail of missing invoices. She would come to me first with a list – five missing. I would scan the paper and, with a feeling of relief say, "I think they're all M's."

Off she would stomp and I'd hear her voice from the barn crying,

"Malcolm! Invoices!"

There was no escape. M would sheepishly go through his pockets and search the floor of the car, finding crumpled bits of paper which he would smooth out to satisfy Dorothy.

My stubborn husband was eventually trained to push all his paperwork onto a spike in the office to keep Dorothy happy.

With more orders going abroad, we had also devised a trademark. Rosecraddoc actually means furse (rhos) and bowl (of land) (craddoc) but it seemed simpler, needing fewer explanations to have a small brass punch engraved with a rose design with UK underneath. This was stamped on the base of all our pots.

The scrunch of car tyres on the gravel drive on our return from that Birmingham show alerted Joyce. She came out to meet us.

"Well how did it go?" Her face was anxious.

"It's ok. Good orders taken and more in the pipeline. We only lost one customer, a Swiss, who sadly said that British goods were now too expensive."

"That's good then, a great relief. I'll leave you two to go and get a cuppa and settle in and I'll tell the others. See you later." And she was gone.

It was an exciting day for Tim and Mark when we told them that we had booked in to an American trade show and that, as it was in August, we'd all be going to New York.

Standby tickets were the cheapest. In those days you could turn up at Heathrow early and take pot luck that a New York flight would have empty seats.

At six in the morning, there was no sign of life at British Airways but both PanAm and T.W.A were wide awake and ready for business. Tickets secured, we went off to have breakfast, Tim deciding to get into the North American mood straight away, ordering maple syrup with his bacon and egg.

Erupting into New York after long hours on the quiet plane we were hit by a wall of noise and rush and heat. We found a low-slung, squashy yellow cab which took us to Columbus Square. The Design Council stands were as usual in a good position under prominent Union Jacks. We were unpacking our samples, which had travelled with us in a suitcase, when I spotted a figure, unmistakeable in any language, coming towards us. The usual stocky figure wearing low-slung jeans and heavy tool belt.

"Look out," I muttered. "This could be trouble."

How wrong I was.

The man's hand stretched out and his round face beamed. "How ya doing? Just wanted to check that all's ok for you folks. D'ya need anything? Extra electrics, lighting? No? Well I'm Al. Here's my card. I'll be over straight away if there is anything, anytime."

He left us breathless at the difference in attitude and with the reassuring feeling that we were all on the same side.

Later, arriving very late, jet-lagged and totally exhausted at the apartment of friends of friends – two dress designers who had, with that open-hearted generosity that Americans are famed for, offered the floor of their design studio for two nights until the accommodation we had rented in Greenwich Village was available. Before settling in, they took us up to their roof garden which overlooked Green Park and its magical, twinkling lights – a host of fireflies, sparkling far below.

This co-operation with union officials continued in the Frankfurt Messe, which we also started attending.

We'd had an idyllic drive along the Rhine. Although it was a cold March day, a pale sun shone on the powerful river with its slow-moving barges and hurtling trains. The road skirted pretty, castellated villages, like something out of Grimms' Fairy Tales. We found a small *gasthof* within striking distance of Frankfurt. A cobbled square, creaking stairs, a wide, polished landing with an ancient, carved bridal chest and downstairs a warm and cosy *wein* bar for supper. A good place for a peaceful night before tackling the city in the morning.

The Messe was very modern, all plate-glass and rippling banners and our first experience of a moving walkway.

In the evenings there was the town to explore, the clattering tram system over cobbled streets and small, steaming restaurants where young girls in dirndl skirts and laced bodices, swung trays of food between crowded tables.

I must have presented a strange figure amongst the sophisticated, smartly-dressed Germans. I had managed to leave my winter coat in the wardrobe of a hotel en route and now had to wear my thickest jersey and my husband's old, padded waistcoat. This ancient item of clothing lived in the back of the car and normally only made its appearance at cattle markets and agricultural fairs.

We arrived at the Messe one morning, in the middle of the show, to find that the shoulder-high, canvas barrier which encircled all British stands overnight, had been broken into. Many companies had lost items from their display and were both annoyed and despondent, lacking samples to show prospective buyers.

Where were the overnight guards?

Was it an inside job?

Once the chatter had died away and business resumed, M and I looked at each other. We had lost nothing, which was good. We still had a complete display. On the other hand, why had nothing been taken? What was wrong with our pots?

Still, orders were good. We built up a useful number of gift shops in Europe, including a well-known French chain store, a beautiful shop in Florence, another chain store in Japan and found an agent, living in Johannesburg, who would sell for us in South Africa.

Returning home, with M driving, I used the time on motorways to sort out orders. Putting them in order of priority, so that we could co-ordinate with orders that had come in while we were away and M could then work out the daily runs of designs. We also discussed new designs and made lists of jobs; new boxes to arrange, visits to the mould maker in Devon and local blacksmith in Gooseberry Lane who made the profiles for the jig and jolley. We always wanted to get back home as soon as possible, retrieve our boys from where they were staying and settle back into our normal domestic routine.

The dreaded 'carnets' were an obstacle to this and caused annoying delays.

A 'carnet' was a document, obtained from Customs and

Excise, which allowed you to transport your products through national boundaries without paying any tax, necessary before the advent of the E.U. and open borders.

All samples had to be listed and the carnet had to be stamped by officials, on each side of a border, so, going into France, going out of France and into Belgium, out of Belgium and so on. At any point you could be stopped and asked to produce your samples to be checked against the list on the carnet.

National characteristics of officials become apparent. The French were light hearted and treated the document as a bit of a joke. The Belgians, scruffy, with newspapers spread on desks, could hardly be bothered. The Germans invariably smart and efficient but sadly unhelpful. My pen broke on one occasion, filling in an extra form for a young, overly officious type but I was curtly refused the loan of his. A kindly lorry driver passed me a biro with a cheery, "Here you are luv."

On this particular journey home, we stopped on the motorway border between Germany and Belgium, on the German side. It was lunch time and all the glass booths that stretched across the *autobahn* were closed, save one, which was staffed by a young, uniformed girl. The queue was long. We eventually reached her and gave her our passports and the carnet. A long sigh. We parked and went to join her in the booth while she telephoned for help. It didn't seem to be forthcoming and between more hopeless sighs, she tried other phone numbers. The queue of cars, wanting to cross the border, grew. M was standing, rather bored but also rather smart in his dark blue blazer and pale shirt. The first motorist looked up and I recognised, with a slight sinking feeling, the gleam in M's eye as a challenge presented itself. He jerked his head. The car drove through, M nodded again and the second car proceeded, unnoticed by the girl who was still struggling with the carnet. This progress continued until the other, more senior officials, having lunch in a building by the side of the barrier, suddenly woke up to what was happening and rushed out.

"Thirteen cars and a motorbike," M announced proudly as we drove away. We managed to wait until we had gone a little distance, before we started laughing.

Chapter 8

Joyce/No More Expansion

Joyce had had an idea. Every so often she spent a couple of hours cutting out small triangles in pot lids so as to accommodate jam spoons. One afternoon she looked at the pile of left-over pieces and said, "What about baking beans?"

It was a good suggestion and M promptly made a few Plaster of Paris moulds, each with a couple of dozen 'bean' holes. Once filled and left to dry, the clay beans were easily lifted out by impressing them with our small brass trademark. They made neat little baking beans and were packed in small bags with our illustrated pottery labels.

We added pie funnels and spoon rests in similar packaging so had a group of inexpensive, stocking-filler type presents which could be displayed by a till and easily added to a shopping basket.

From time to time at trade shows we had been approached by major UK companies, either wanting us to design a special range or supply them with our existing designs. Once, it was an American department store chain who wanted our entire range but in their own design packaging. These were tempting offers and would lift us into another business category where we would be competing with the largest commercial potteries. An interesting and exciting challenge, but did we want it?

We looked at the implications. Major investment would be needed, also larger premises as we had been told that, at Rosecraddoc, despite upgrades, we were on the limit of our power supply. We would also need more staff and more equipment. We had never had a large overdraft and debt frightened us. When this type of expansion is based on a single customer, a business is entering dangerous territory. We had heard of huge orders delivered and then returned intact because of one, minor fault within a carton pulled out at random for inspection. With our sort of 'hand-made' pottery, despite our own tight quality control, minor differences in pots were inevitable, they were part of the charm and faults were subjective. With such a large sum of money at risk, the return of an order could easily cause bankruptcy.

The stores also realise how dependent you are on their large orders and they sometimes use this knowledge to drive down prices, demanding larger and larger discounts. We had seen other companies take this road and didn't want the stress involved – to lose control and be forced to take virtually any order to keep staff occupied. Such widespread availability of our products would probably also result in losing our best quality, individual outlets.

Beside, we didn't want to move. We loved working at Rosecraddoc and enjoyed the tight-knit group of people that we had working for us. It was a good way of life and we didn't want to do anything to endanger it.

It is very difficult though to maintain a company at a particular size – one is usually either growing or shrinking. Our policy, gradually arrived at, was to produce a quality product, supplied to the best outlet in each town. Cities could take more than one shop but never too close together. We decided to export as much as possible and keep the range fresh with new designs.

Sometimes we would receive criticism – I loathe the culture of envy still prevalent in this country – anti-business, anti-profit, anti-success. We would be told, "It's all right for people like you. You're the lucky ones." Looking at our lifestyle and working hours compared to their 9-5 with a guaranteed cheque at the end of the month, it didn't seem particularly lucky but we wouldn't have changed a thing.

It's hugely sad that young people are not encouraged to set their sights high, to follow their passions and relish their opportunities. You only live once!

Mark was into natural history. Despite having the smallest bedroom he managed to cram it full of specimens and other objects. He even had charts on the ceiling. He had a microscope and dissected anything he could find that looked interesting and reconstructed the skeletons of small mammals found within owl turds, mounting them on sheets of card. He collected minerals from the spoil heaps of old mines up on the moor and, when he was uncertain what they were, sent them off to the Natural History Museum for identification. Finding a dead heron in good condition, he started taxidermy... Our chest freezer lived in the open linhay at the side of the house and local farmers and friends, finding unusual birds and animals, would pop them into the freezer for Mark. Once, going there for a Sunday joint and lifting the lid, I jumped back when I found a badger staring at me.

Somehow, word of Mark's activities spread and first an article appeared in *Cornish Life*, then a team from our local BBC TV visited. I've said that Mark's room was the smallest – an interviewer plus equipment was squeezed in but spotlights and the two cameramen had to operate from the landing. At the end of the proceedings, the cameraman panned back slowly, concentrating so hard that he didn't realise his backside was against a spotlight until smoke and a lick of flame set him leaping, whacking his bottom. Fortunately his trousers were thick and we managed to beat out the flames before damage was done. His colleague was inconsolable that he hadn't managed to film the incident for an 'out-take' programme.

Chapter 9

The Margarets/Falklands War/Weekend Break

The pottery had acquired two naval wives, both called Margaret. The Falklands War was beginning, the task force was on its way to the South Atlantic and the Margarets were looking for distraction whilst their husbands were at sea. Lively and able, they were an enormous asset and good company.

The radio was always on in the pottery, Radio 2 in the morning with Terry Wogan, followed by Jimmy Young, complete with the popular Legal Beagle and 'Recipe for Today'. M had his choice of Radio 3 in the afternoon. News bulletins were listened to anxiously and M kept the Margarets as busy as possible.

We were particularly glad to have them as we had been having a difficult time finding reliable help. Young people weren't interested in an eight o'clock start and the half an hour walk from either Liskeard or St. Cleer was too much for them. We even offered second-hand bikes but had had no success recruiting.

As M and I have totally different methods of working, to preserve marital relations we had divided the business into two parts. M ran the manufacturing side and I took the finished pots, made up orders and did the marketing.

The pottery had spread. The old hay store with its slate floor and stone walls was now the office where Dorothy and a part-time secretary worked. The dairy housed the gate-leg dining room table, rarely used these days, and took overflow equipment and storage. Then came the barn with its cob walls and old rat holes. We still used the first, small, second-hand kiln, found in a field and bought for twenty five pounds, with its tangle of hanging wire elements which never would stay in their slots and which had to be replaced regularly, but this little kiln had some sentimental value and was still useful for test firings. Another, larger kiln stood in a corner and was used for biscuit firings. There was a long table under the window for fettling and glazing and my father's 'industrial shelf' where we stored items not in daily use. The barn led into the new extension with its two new kilns, the jig and jolley, drying cupboard – still the same old wardrobe with an extra piece – and more work tables and storage racks. Also, a useful piece of equipment called a 'pug' which pulverised waste clay in a sort of giant mincing machine and extruded a long sausage of good, smooth clay ready to use again.

Once the pots had been glazed and had had their second firing, they came through to my territory. Joyce was usually the one who wrapped them in tissue, placed them in gift boxes then stacked them on metal shelves ready for orders. The orders, of course, were made up in the packing room which I've already described.

Tim had decided to follow a favourite uncle into estate management so was working hard for his 'A' levels, hoping to do a degree. He also wanted a social life and, with some school friends, had discovered a night club in Union Street, Plymouth. Not the most desirable area but we couldn't coddle him so, with some strict rules and emergency money in his sock, off he went. The first night, catching the milk train home, he fell deeply asleep and didn't wake up until he was well past Liskeard. After that he carried a small alarm clock which got him off at the right station but which was not popular with other recumbent revellers going further down the line.

Mark, at fifteen, wanted a holiday job, ideally in a photographers, one of his main interests, but in reality anything which would earn him some money. He sat for two hours one morning with the telephone book, eventually wandering into the kitchen.

"It's no good," he said despondently. "There's nothing doing, anywhere."

"Come and have a coffee," I suggested. "Then perhaps you could give it another go."

Half an hour later he was jubilant. A fisherman's cafe on the quay in West Looe had offered him work, five or six mornings a week. The only problem was a 6am start. My lie-a-bed son, who liked to stay under his duvet until the last possible moment, managed to get himself up at 5am, cycle into Liskeard, catch the early train down to Looe and walk over to West Looe for 6 o'clock.

He held the job for a couple of summers, earned good money and tips and was never late once.

We tried to look after our staff; after all, it was in our own interests. Apart from the fact that it's pleasant working with people who are happy with their conditions and way of work, you retain your people and they will go out of their way to help you and vice versa. It all seems so logical but it's amazing how many businesses don't follow this easy recipe.

M's brother, Rodney, very generously audited our accounts every year in exchange for a porcelain bird to add to his collection. He liked to analyse our range and point out the more profitable lines, doing his best to discourage us from making the less financially rewarding. Our wine cooler was a constant irritant. Wine coolers were suddenly in vogue and M had produced an attractive design of vines, encircling the cylindrical pot, the leaves hanging from a shallow, horizontal groove. The item sold well.

Terracotta is ideal for use as a cooler as, once soaked in water, the evaporation both reduces and keeps the temperature down. This useful property was traditionally used to cool both butter and milk.

Rodney's criticism was that wine coolers didn't make much of a profit and should be discontinued. Our point was that:

1. They were popular.
2. They made an attractive display and drew the eye.
3. Buyers were more inclined to order our range with wine coolers included.

The argument went on... Sometimes, M and I decided a design had to be appreciated as a bit of a loss leader.

We had had a particularly stressful few weeks. An order from the box company had arrived at the last minute, following increasingly frantic phone calls as a deadline approached, with the lid design printed upside down. Work that had to be re-done. I hated letting customers down.

There was an ongoing problem with clay supplies. The bags looked completely normal in the raw state but, once fired, the material was spotted and couldn't be glazed properly. Contamination was obviously occurring but was hard to trace and a lot of waste was occurring. Compensation for the faulty bags of clay didn't begin to cover our lost production and expenses.

Also, a shipping company had delivered a substantial consignment to our American agent in Dallas, Texas, without waiting for word from us that payment had been cleared. It was a large sum of money and I had attempted to hold the shipping company responsible without success. I then had the unenviable job of ringing the agent daily, requesting payment.

The agent was a young Englishman. An over-the-top 'deb's delight' and a great hit with the Americans because of this – I think they thought he was royalty. I was relieved when, after several weeks of almost daily verbal fencing and a huge phone bill, our money arrived.

Others weren't so lucky and, at the next trade show, Top Drawer in Kensington, word went around that he was black-listed. Eventually he went bankrupt.

M and I were so tired – we needed a break but were too exhausted to contemplate planning one. Dorothy found us in the kitchen one lunch time.

"You're off on Friday," she announced, "no excuses. The boys are old enough to look after themselves for a weekend and I've found a pub in the *Good Pub Guide* and booked you in for a couple of nights. It's called The Nobody Inn," she laughed, "in a place called Doddyscombleigh, in Devon."

It was heaven, with perfect weather thrown in as a bonus. We stayed in the old rectory which the pub owners had just finished renovating – we had a pale, beautifully proportioned room and followed a path through a hay field in the sun to find a drink.

We paused in the porch and watched swallows darting up to their nests under a beam, breathing in the scent of roses and honeysuckle.

"We're a bit early," said M doubtfully, looking at his watch. "I wonder what time they open."

The oak door stood ajar and the response came swiftly.

"6 o'clock but do come in and have a drink while you are waiting."

The Nobody Inn became a favourite escape – good food and a list of two hundred wines and forty whiskies. The countryside around, bordering the Wray Valley with views of the high moor, was breathtakingly beautiful. There were also good walks around the reservoirs of Trenchfold, Tottifold and Kennick.

The nearby village of Lustleigh was another special haunt. We had met a friendly couple at the Torquay spring show who had a small gallery in the village and, whenever an order was needed, we tried to snatch a day off and deliver it personally.

The village was picture perfect; thatched cottages round a green, another delightful pub, a cricket field and an award winning tea room. The discovery of this village was to play a big part in our lives before too long.

The dreadful suspense of the Falklands War was finally over and our forces began to make their way home.

The husband of one of the Margarets, Chief Petty Officer on *HMS Brilliant*, was expected shortly and one morning Margaret rang in to say that the ship was due to dock and she was off to Plymouth to meet her husband.

I ran through the pottery to tell them all the good news.

"Right. That's it," said M, chucking his ball of clay back into the bag. "We're all going to Plymouth. We'll join the crowds on the Hoe and cheer them in."

It was a long wait in a biting wind. A multitude of small boats jostled in the huge harbour. Tugs, pilot boats, fire-tenders, all manoeuvred out by the breakwater.

We stamped up and down and wrapped our arms round our bodies in an effort to stay warm, chatting and speculating with others in the large crowd as we waited. A speck appeared, rounding Rame Head. So small. Could it possibly be? Binoculars were raised – an anxious peering – then a confident shout. "It's them. It's them!" And a tidal wave of sound travelled out, over the grey sea. A sound of ships whooping, sirens hooting, arching water spouts from the tenders as the small, travel-stained ship was escorted home.

Children leapt and capered, waving their flags and shouting while the adults clapped and cheered with tears running down their cold cheeks.

Chapter 10

The End

There had been an on-going problem – a worsening problem as far as we were concerned, with the wood – this lovely, quiet planting of tall conifers, rookerys, crimson rhododendron and the rare, native daffodil that our cottage faced into.

The Rosecraddoc Estate had been bought by a London entrepreneur who had obtained permission to develop the woodland as a holiday park. The whole area, we had previously been told, was to be scheduled as an area of Outstanding Natural Beauty but this never happened and building began.

The first twelve bungalows were down at the far end of the wood, some distance away, and life continued much as before. The next fifty came towards us rapidly. It hurt, almost physically, to hear the chain saws and to see those trees, some planted in the nineteenth century from seed sent by early plant hunters, wrenched from their roots. To hear the crashes as the glorious Cornish reds (*rhododendron arboreum*), which had made such a wonderful crimson tunnel of the long drive through the woods, hit the ground. The noise and disruption came ever closer – cement mixers churning, men shouting and lorries revving, tipping their loads of concrete blocks.

Very suddenly, it seemed, the finished bungalows appeared right across the bottom of the garden. Our peace and privacy was gone.

The stable block by the manor had been turned into a nightclub and summer nights were disturbed by carousers returning through the woods in the early hours. One night, yet again, we were woken by screams. This time the screams sounded desperate, as if a girl was in serious trouble. M leapt out of bed and rushed to the window.

"Are you all right?" he yelled. "D'you need help?" A pause and then a loud volley of abuse from both parties.

It was exhausting and upsetting.

That year, it must have been the late eighties, was a particularly lovely summer and we all used to take our mugs of morning coffee into the garden. Some days, ten minutes was just not long enough and we would take another ten and sit and savour the peaceful scene. On those days, come four o'clock and going home time, our wonderful workers would say,

"Oh no. You gave us extra time this morning – we'll do a bit more now."

We were sitting in the garden one morning, chit-chatting casually, watching the fish lazily circling in the pond and admiring the blooms on the old roses I had planted among the apple trees. We realised that, instead of bird song and the occasional snuffling of pigs from the sty, we were being assaulted by pop music coming from three different directions.

"You're not going to be able to stay here you know," Joyce remarked.

The words fell into a void, a long silence. M and I looked at each other – we were thinking the unthinkable. This was Rosecraddoc. We belonged. It was where we had brought up our children. We loved everything about the place – its essence in the sweet, old smell when we re-entered the cottage after an absence. But the unthinkable stayed with us. We mentioned the possibility of a move, cautiously, to the boys, expecting that they would be both appalled and upset.

"Wow!"

"How exciting!" was their response.

"Where are we going?"

Where? That was a good question. Not only would we have to find somewhere to live but we would have to find another source of income.

"Time we had another night at The Nobody and a good long walk," suggested M.

After the walk around the peaceful paths of the three reservoirs, we drove down to the pretty, thatched village of Lustleigh for a sandwich in the pub beside the green. We sat in the garden enjoying the sun. A track ran down to the cricket field and across the track stood a large, stone built house with a 'FOR SALE' sign, hanging above the gate.

It was a good-looking house on three floors, built by a stone mason for his own occupation. With six bedrooms, it had possibilities – maybe a Bed and Breakfast? Would we get permission?

The pottery was on the market, advertised in *Dalton's Weekly* as we had decided to sell it ourselves. It seemed that everyone liked the idea of having a pottery in Cornwall and we were flooded with enquiries and visits from prospective purchasers.

The planning department in Devon made discouraging noises about a Bed and Breakfast in Lustleigh but they didn't say no. We would have to wait until the next meeting.

The 'flood' of prospective purchasers whittled down to two or three serious buyers and eventually a price and a completion date was agreed.

Ray, our London agent, was something of a railway enthusiast. Browsing through Great Western pamphlets from the 1920s one day, he came across the Lustleigh house advertising B & B. This gave us a precedent and there were no further problems with the planners.

After that, it all seemed to happen rather quickly.

The day the removal van arrived, I felt suspended from reality, all feeling gone, as if in a dream. Nothing seemed quite real – even sound was deadened.

M worried, I think, that I would suddenly refuse to go. He hustled things along, joking with the removal men as they manoeuvred the upstairs furniture down through the coffin hole in the sitting-room ceiling and phoning the new owners to say that we would be gone in an hour.

An hour! Reality hit. Tim disappeared for a reflective walk around the garden, Mark went in search of Mitzi who always ran off at signs of travel and I began to collect the remaining small objects that were to go with us in the car.

At last all was stowed. The picnic basket was packed. A last look around the kitchen – scene of so many family meals, suppers with friends, late night plans and decisions round the old trestle table.

The heavily laden car drove off with its cargo of silent passengers.

Don't look back.

No regrets.

We're just off on another adventure.

Guidelines:

There are many ways of starting a business – this is what worked for us.

- Start evenings and weekends while doing the day job – for security in case your idea doesn't work.

- Borrow nothing or as little as possible – a shed/outbuilding is better than paying for shiny new premises on an industrial estate.

- Second hand/reconditioned machinery is often good value for money.

- 'Rush' difficult/unpleasant jobs, i.e. tackle them first thing in the morning when you are fresh, then they don't hang over you all day.

- When debt collecting on the phone, distance yourself from the problem by saying, "I'm afraid my accountant insists on payment within 30 days," or, "My accountant is on my back so I can't let this go on any longer." Putting all the blame on your accountant (who may be entirely fictional) helps to keep your relations sweet with the customer.

- Look after your customers and keep them in touch with what's happening. For instance, if there's a long lead time on their order, telephone to reassure them that it's on track and will be delivered on the due date.

- Keep in touch, particularly if something goes wrong. Customers are more likely to be tolerant of a late delivery if you have warned them of a problem.

- Keep suppliers on your side. Always give special thanks when they have made a special effort.

- Share stands at exhibitions to reduce costs, although, as the business grows, you need to stand alone to be taken seriously.

- Always design and set up your stand at home first so that you only transport what is necessary and you know exactly what is going where.

- Good lighting is essential. Make sure that you have ordered enough power points.

- Treat your staff well. Make sure that working conditions are as pleasant as possible and that they have somewhere comfortable for their breaks. Explain what is happening and why you are doing things the way you do. Ask for their suggestions and ideas – involve them in the business.

- Use your buyers as sources of information – what are they looking for? – how do they see trends? – ask them to recommend good agents.

- Keep all receipts – keep bookkeepers happy!

Above all, quoting the businessman, Sir John Harvey-Jones, "Always look for ways to reduce costs and maximise profits."

...and if you ever do start your own business...

Good Luck!

M and J